STATE
OF AFFAIRS:
NATIVE AMERICANS
IN THE 21ST CENTURY

NATIVE AMERICANS
AND THE
US GOVERNMENT

JOANNE MATTERN

Mitchell Lane
PUBLISHERS

P.O. Box 196
Hockessin, Delaware 19707
Visit us on the web: www.mitchelllane.com
Comments? Email us: mitchelllane@mitchelllane.com

STATE OF AFFAIRS:
NATIVE AMERICANS
IN THE 21ST CENTURY

Preserving Their Heritage
Native Americans and the US Government
Native American Industry in Contemporary America
Life on the Reservations

PUBLISHER'S NOTE: The facts on which the story in this book is based have been thoroughly researched. Documentation of such research can be found on page 44. While every possible effort has been made to ensure accuracy, the publisher will not assume liability for damages caused by inaccuracies in the data, and makes no warranty on the accuracy of the information contained herein.

ABOUT THE AUTHOR:
Joanne Mattern has loved American history since she was a little girl. She has written many books about American history and culture and contributed to an encyclopedia of American immigration. Joanne has also written numerous biographies of major historical figures such as Sam Houston, Barack Obama, William Penn, and several first ladies. Joanne lives in New York State with her husband and four children and spends a lot of time at her local library.

Printing   1   2   3   4   5   6   7   8   9

Library of Congress
Cataloging-in-Publication Data
Mattern, Joanne, 1963-
 Native Americans and the government / by Joanne Mattern.
    pages cm. — (State of affairs: Native Americans in the 21st century)
 Includes bibliographical references and index.
 ISBN 978-1-61228-442-2 (library bound)
 1. Indians of North America—Government relations. 2. Indians of North America—Politics and government. 3. Indians of North America—Social conditions. I. Title.
 E93.M455 2013
 323.1197—dc23
                                        2013012559

eBook ISBN: 9781612285030

PLB

CONTENTS

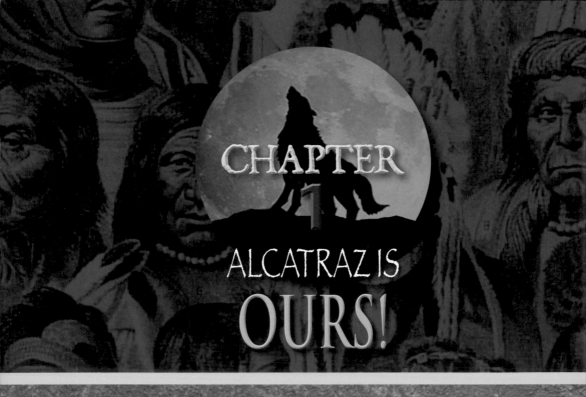

CHAPTER 1

ALCATRAZ IS

OURS!

For many years, Alcatraz was known and feared as "The Rock." This desolate island off the coast of San Francisco, California, was used as a prison by the federal government. Hundreds of dangerous criminals were imprisoned there. The island was so isolated that only a few people ever tried to escape, and nobody is sure that anyone ever succeeded.

Alcatraz prison was closed in 1963. A few years later, the rocky island became known for something much more hopeful and important. A deserted island might seem like a strange place for a group of Native Americans to take a stand, but that's exactly what happened. The prison became the site of a Native American occupation that would change the way people and the government viewed native tribes.

By the 1960s, Native Americans had endured almost two hundred years of difficulties with the United States government. The 1960s were a time of social unrest and change. Many different groups, including African Americans, Hispanics, and

Between 1934 and 1963, Alcatraz Island was considered the toughest prison in the United States. Many dangerous criminals were housed there, and escape was nearly impossible because the prison was surrounded by the fast, violent currents of the San Francisco Bay. After its occupation by Native Americans in 1964 and 1969, Alcatraz became a popular tourist attraction.

Only five members of the Sioux tribe occupied Alcatraz Island in 1964, and their efforts only lasted a few hours. Just five years later, however, the island would be the site of a much larger and more historic Native American occupation.

women, were fighting for their rights. It was the perfect time for Native Americans to speak up too.

The first occupation of Alcatraz occurred in 1964, soon after the prison closed and the federal government abandoned the island. That year, a Sioux woman named Belva Cottier read a treaty between the Sioux and the US government that was signed in 1868. According to this treaty, the Sioux had the right to reclaim unused land that had been taken from them by the federal government. Cottier decided that this meant that the Sioux had the right to live on Alcatraz.

Cottier explained her idea to five Sioux men; they agreed to give the idea a try. On March 9, 1964, the five men took a boat to Alcatraz. When they arrived, they drove claim sticks into the ground and declared that a Native American cultural center and university should be established on the island. The men remained on the island for only four hours, but their work was not finished. One of the men, Richard McKenzie, went to court to try to claim the official title to the island. However, it soon became clear that the original treaty referred to land that was near the Great Sioux Reservation in South Dakota, not an isolated island off the coast of California.

Even though the 1964 occupation did not really change anything, Native Americans were not finished with the idea. On November 20, 1969, a more ambitious effort to reclaim the island began. Several dozen Native American college students arrived on Alcatraz to begin another occupation of the island. This time, the occupation lasted more than a year and a half.

Occupiers turned Alcatraz's empty prison cells into residences during their time on the island.

A Native American teepee was set up on Alcatraz Island during the 1969 occupation, creating an unusual view of San Francisco Bay.

At first the occupiers wanted to develop several Native American cultural institutions on the island, such as a spiritual center and a museum. However, the students had a greater reason for occupying Alcatraz. They wanted to draw attention to the poor treatment that Native Americans had endured at the hands of the US government. For years, the government had broken treaties and promises with Native Americans. Most recently, the native people were angry at the loss of tribal lands that occurred as the federal government began moving residents of Indian reservations into urban areas and taking away their land.

The group that arrived on the island called itself Indians of All Tribes. Their leader was Richard Oakes, a student at a San Francisco college. He and his friends were aided by dozens of supporters who helped the effort from their homes. People who lived in San Francisco and the surrounding area generally sympathized with the Native Americans' cause. At the time, San Francisco was the center of the counterculture, a movement that spoke out against and defied authority. The Native Americans' efforts came at the right time and location.

At first, the US government tried to remove the occupiers. The government sent Coast Guard boats to blockade the island and keep supporters and supplies from reaching Alcatraz. The FBI got involved and planned to storm the island and remove the protesters by force. However, President Richard Nixon stepped in and told authorities to leave the occupiers alone. For the next nineteen months, the occupiers were free to stay on the island. Supporters came and went. The island's population was at its peak on November 27, 1969, when four hundred people celebrated Thanksgiving on the island.

The recreation yard at Alcatraz became the site of a huge Thanksgiving feast for hundreds of occupiers in November of 1969.

Alcatraz

By June 11, 1971, only about fifteen people remained on the island. At that point, US Marshals and FBI agents raided Alcatraz and removed the Native Americans. The occupation of Alcatraz was officially over. But everything had changed. The occupation had brought the attention of the whole nation to the difficulties that Native Americans faced. For the first time, the public and the media were aware of how Native Americans had been treated by the government. During the occupation, President Nixon ended the US tribal termination policy of removing natives from reservations. Many Native American leaders felt this action was a direct result of the Alcatraz occupation.

Actor Benjamin Bratt and his brother were children at the time of the occupation. Their mother, a Native American from Peru, had brought them to live on the island for a time. Years after the event, the brothers said, "Forty years later, Native people still recognize the occupation for what it was and remains: a seminal event in American history that brought the plight of American Indians to the world's attention."[1]

The occupation of Alcatraz helped ignite the important "Red Power" movement of the 1970s. This movement was an effort to win freedom and fair treatment from the government. But it was just one moment in a long battle between Native Americans and the US government that had been going on since the first European settlers arrived in the New World.

BELVA COTTIER
SPEAKS

In a 1979 interview, Belva Cottier explained what happened during the 1964 occupation of Alcatraz Island:

We told the young Indians from the [San Francisco American Indian Center] that we were going to do something and to meet us in costume. There were five of us Sioux, and we actually had claim sticks to do it like Lewis and Clark did . . . We had notified Washington of our plans but they didn't respond and after we gathered on Pier 41 . . . we called the news media and said, "We're going to claim Alcatraz." Only about ten people from the newspapers showed up. They didn't believe us . . . We went to the island's west side . . . but there was a guard there with a police dog telling us, "Don't you know that you aren't allowed within two hundred feet of the island?" We went around to the east side . . . and jumped off. Each of the Sioux men with a claim stick dashed off to put it on different parts of the 12 ½ acres. The rest started singing victory songs . . .

The officials were still on the island, so the Sioux leader read them the proclamation claiming the island as Indian land for all tribes. The official telephoned the Federal Marshal . . . "There are Indians on the island, feathers, bells and all." . . . We were advised to stay until we could meet with the US Marshal, but somehow this was never accomplished. But we felt that we had completed our mission by testing the 1868 treaty . . . We loaded up and went back to shore.[2]

Belva Cottier

CHAPTER 2
NEW
RULES

Large numbers of Europeans began settling North America during the 1600s. Long before they arrived, Native Americans lived there. Then commonly called Indians, historians estimate that between two and eighteen million of them lived in North America before European settlement. These native people belonged to a large number of tribes, scattered from the northeast down to the deep south and as far west as the Pacific coast. Each tribe was different from the others, with its own language, culture, and traditions.

The Native Americans lived a very different lifestyle than the Europeans did. During those early days, most Native Americans were nomads. They moved with the seasons or followed the animals they hunted. Individual people or tribes did not own land. The concept of ownership was completely unknown to the natives. Instead, they believed that land and all the animals and plants on it were resources to be shared and respected by everyone.

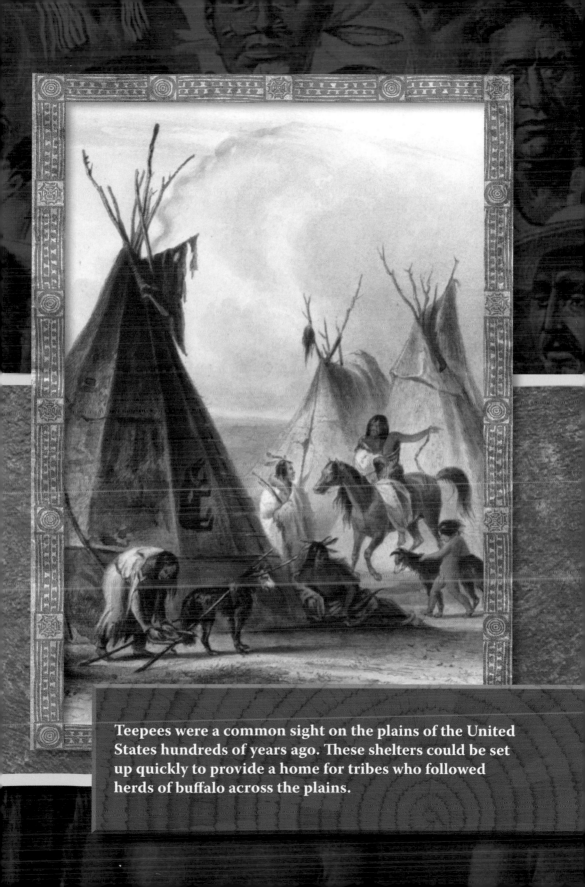

Teepees were a common sight on the plains of the United States hundreds of years ago. These shelters could be set up quickly to provide a home for tribes who followed herds of buffalo across the plains.

The Europeans had a very different perspective. For Europeans, owning land was an important sign of wealth. The more land someone controlled, the more powerful and rich he could be. Europeans also viewed the land and its resources as theirs for the taking. They were eager to control the wealth in the New World, from the rich timber of its forests to the furs of its animals, and from the abundant farmland to the riches of the minerals hidden under the ground.

At first, relations between the European newcomers and the natives were pretty peaceful. Land and natural resources were plentiful enough for everyone. The Europeans also brought goods that the natives had never seen before, including guns, gunpowder, and metal tools. Native Americans were eager to trade their goods for these new objects. Many times, the natives helped the settlers survive in this strange new world.

As time went on and the number of settlers grew, things changed. Many of the Europeans believed that they were better than the Native Americans. They also believed that they had the right to take what they wanted. If the Native Americans were living on land that the settlers wanted, well, too bad for the natives.

Another complication was the government itself. Because different areas of North America were settled by different European nations—including Great Britain, Holland, Spain, and France—there was no consistent policy toward the Native Americans. North America was a huge land, and the settlers in different places wanted and needed different things from the natives. These different needs created different beliefs and policies.

Things got even more complicated when war broke out between the newly declared nation of the United States and Great Britain in 1776. At that time, colonists worried that the Indians might side with the British against the Americans, because Great Britain's policies toward Native Americans were more generous than the ones adopted by the colonies. Their

Joseph Brant was a Mohawk chief who supported the British during the French and Indian War (1754-1763). He and his tribe supported the British again during the American Revolution, often attacking American soldiers. The Mohawks were given land in Ontario, Canada, where Brant died in 1807.

fears were realized when the powerful Mohawk tribe in the northeastern United States did side with the British. Other tribes sided with the colonists, however, leading to battles between tribes as well as between colonial forces and British soldiers.

After the United States won its independence from Great Britain and officially became a nation in 1783, the new nation claimed all the land from the Atlantic Ocean all the way to the Mississippi River in the west; from the Great Lakes in the north to Georgia in the south. The new government said that since the Native Americans had fought with the British, they were a

Although Native Americans had lived in villages like these for centuries, settlers from Europe did not think the land belonged to the natives and did everything they could to force the Native Americans to leave.

conquered nation and had no rights in the new land. The Indians who had fought with the United States were conveniently forgotten.

As the years passed, the government's policies toward the Native Americans changed as the needs of the country changed. For example, if gold was discovered on land where Native Americans lived, the United States government would take the land so they could mine the gold. These complicated changes meant that there was never one consistent policy toward the Native Americans. That led to a lot of trouble later on.

President George Washington and Henry Knox, the secretary of war, believed that the Native Americans would eventually have two choices to survive. They could either become part of society in the United States, or sell their land to the settlers and move further west to continue hunting for food. The second possibility seemed like a good idea to Washington and Knox because it would allow settlers to take over new land without having to fight the Indians or go through any legal action to obtain it.

Some Native Americans did move west to find better hunting. However, others were reluctant to leave the places where they and their families had lived for many years. As the number of settlers grew and the American nation also expanded, things got even more complicated. It wasn't long before the government started to pass laws that created huge disruptions in native life.

GEORGE WASHINGTON'S POLICY TOWARD NATIVE AMERICANS

Soon after he took office as president, George Washington stated his intention to create a fair policy toward Indians. He explained that the government was determined that its dealings with natives would be guided by the principles of justice and humanity. Washington also stated that all arrangements with Native Americans would be spelled out in treaties, just as the United States arranged treaties with foreign countries like Great Britain and France.

It became clear, however, that Washington would have to use force to get the Indians to accept American settlement. When Native Americans grew angry at the constant flow of white settlers invading their lands, Washington saw protecting American citizens as his most important duty. Beginning in 1790, Washington sent armies to put down conflicts between natives and United States settlers.

By 1796, Washington and the rest of the government realized that they were not the ones making the rules when it came to Indian territories. Those rules were being made by the settlers swarming westward. As Washington wrote, "I believe scarcely anything short of a Chinese wall, or a line of troops, will restrain land jobbers, and the encroachment of settlers upon the Indian territory."[1]

George Washington

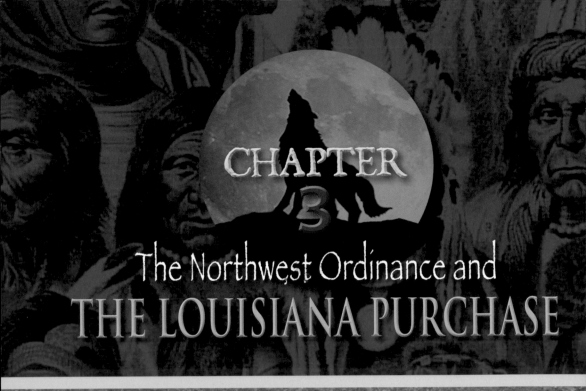

CHAPTER 3

The Northwest Ordinance and
THE LOUISIANA PURCHASE

In 1787, the United States government made its first effort to legislate how it would deal with native peoples. Congress passed a law called the Northwest Ordinance. This document stated, "The utmost good faith shall always be observed towards the Indians; their lands and property shall never be taken from them without their consent; and in their property, rights, and liberty, they shall never be invaded or disturbed, unless in just and lawful wars authorized by Congress; but laws founded in justice and humanity shall from time to time be made, for preventing wrongs being done to them, and for preserving peace and friendship with them."[1] This law sounds fair and straightforward. Unfortunately, the people who lived in the United States did not pay much attention to it.

Most American settlers had no intention of respecting Indian rights. If they wanted a piece of land, they moved in and took it. It didn't matter to the settlers that the Indians were there first or that the law said that Native Americans had to agree to

Chief Oshkosh, whose statue is shown here, faced a problem common to many tribal leaders during the 1800s. He tried to negotiate a fair treaty between his Menominee tribe and the US government but was forced to give up most of his tribe's land in what is now the state of Wisconsin.

give up their land and receive a fair price for it. Settlers were not willing to wait until Native Americans moved away, as Washington and Knox had hoped.

It didn't take long for violence to break out between Native Americans and settlers. In 1790, Indian tribes including the Shawnee, Miami, Potawatomi, and Ojibwa united under Chief Little Turtle to defend their land in the Ohio Valley. The united tribes defeated 1,400 soldiers commanded by General Josiah Harmar. After the defeat, the US government sent another army led by General Arthur St. Clair. The Native Americans also defeated that army. Finally, in 1794, Major General Anthony Wayne led a force of three thousand soldiers and defeated the Indians. The tribes had to give up most of their land, as well as the rights to land north of the Ohio River and east of the Mississippi River. That territory would later become the state of Ohio.

Events took an even more dramatic turn in 1804 when President Thomas Jefferson purchased a huge tract of land from France. This became known as the Louisiana Purchase, and the United States doubled in size. Now the United States had plenty of land . . . and plenty of places to move Native Americans.

Until the Louisiana Purchase, the American government had been more interested in getting native people to assimilate into American culture. The plan was that Native Americans would learn to accept European culture and religion. They would give up their own traditions, languages, and religious beliefs and become absorbed into United States society. In 1803, Jefferson wrote a document called "Policy of Civilization and Assimilation" which stated, "the ultimate point of rest and happiness for them is to let our settlements and theirs meet and blend together, to intermix, and become one people . . . Incorporating themselves with us as citizens of the United States, this is what the natural progress of things will, of course, bring on . . . Surely it will be better for them to be identified with us, and preserved in the occupation of their lands, than be exposed to the many casualties which may endanger them while a separate people . . . "[2]

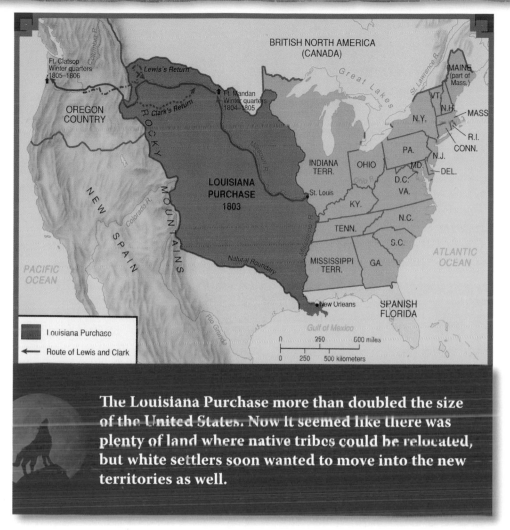

The Louisiana Purchase more than doubled the size of the United States. Now it seemed like there was plenty of land where native tribes could be relocated, but white settlers soon wanted to move into the new territories as well.

After the Louisiana Purchase, however, moving the Native Americans off of their lands was possible and became a popular idea. Indians would be removed from their lands in the north and east and sent to lands that were reserved for them in the wilderness areas of the west.

Jefferson began to negotiate with tribes that lived between the Appalachian Mountains and the Mississippi River, encouraging them to move to the Louisiana Territory. However, these tribes were not interested. Instead, Jefferson and the presidents who followed him turned to treaties to get the land they wanted.

President Thomas Jefferson hired Meriwether Lewis and William Clark to explore the new lands of the Louisiana Purchase. Along the way, Lewis and Clark met many native tribes. This painting shows the explorers entering a Native American village in the western United States.

Many of these treaties were agreements for the natives to sell their land to the government. Many tribal chiefs were eager to take the large amounts of money the government was offering. Other chiefs were bribed with additional money or land to persuade them to sign treaties. Sometimes treaties were signed by people who did not even have the power to represent their tribes.

When treaties and bribes did not work, military action was usually the next option. In 1824, the Bureau of Indian Affairs, or BIA, was formed as part of the War Department. As settlers took over Indian land, Native Americans used force to reclaim it. Once this happened, the US government would send in troops to protect its citizens—and remove the Native Americans from their land.

While many tribes did give up their lands, others would not go down without a fight. The southern United States was home to the powerful Cherokee, Creek, Chickasaw, and Seminole tribes. These tribes refused to sign treaties or give up their land. They demanded that the United States honor earlier treaties that had promised the Indians could stay on their land. By 1830, a confrontation was brewing that would change the face of US-Indian relations forever.

THE BUREAU OF INDIAN AFFAIRS

Originally, Indian relations with the US government were the responsibility of the Continental Congress. In 1775, the Committee on Indian Affairs was created, headed by Benjamin Franklin. In 1824, Secretary of War John Calhoun established the Bureau of Indian Affairs, better known as the BIA, which would be responsible for creating treaties and trade agreements with the tribes. After being part of the Department of War for twenty-five years, the BIA was transferred to the US Department of the Interior in 1849.

The BIA's mission has changed over the years as government policies and attitudes changed. From forcing Indians to give up their culture to returning self-determination to native tribes, the BIA has been faced with the impossible job of trying to make everyone happy. At first there were no Native Americans in the BIA, but eventually natives gained representation in the Bureau. However, over the years, the BIA has been accused of corruption and activities that benefitted individuals rather than tribes. Although the Bureau states that its mission is "to enhance the quality of life, to promote economic opportunity, and to carry out the responsibility to protect and improve the trust assets of American Indians, Indian tribes, and Alaska Natives,"[3] few people would say that it has been successful in achieving these goals.

Benjamin Franklin

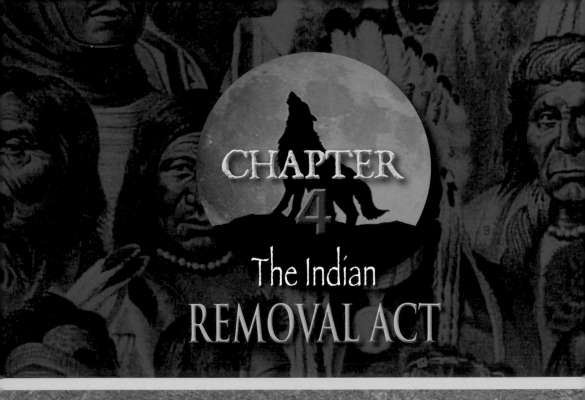

CHAPTER 4
The Indian REMOVAL ACT

In 1829, President Andrew Jackson took office. He proved to be a major force behind removing Native Americans from their lands. Before he became president, Jackson had commanded forces against native tribes in several wars. Now he was about to force his will on the Indians with the full power of the government behind him.

The Cherokee tribe turned to the courts to try to save their land. Back in 1827, the Cherokee had declared themselves to be a sovereign nation which could make treaties with the United States. In 1830, the Cherokee tried to use this status in court. They asked the state of Georgia for legal protection from white settlers who were attacking Native Americans and taking their lands. When Georgia refused, the Cherokee took their case all the way to the US Supreme Court. The Supreme Court ruled against them.

Despite this loss, the Cherokee did not give up. They went back to the Supreme Court in 1831 to appeal the court's decision.

President Andrew Jackson believed that relocating Native Americans was the only way for white settlers to obtain their own land. He led many violent campaigns to remove natives from their land. Here President Jackson accepts the surrender of Red Eagle, a famous Creek chief.

In 1830, a law had been passed in Georgia which required whites to have a license from the state in order to live in Indian territories. The Cherokee based their appeal on this law. This, of course, was not what the state had intended when the law was written. Georgia had hoped to remove white missionaries who were helping the Cherokee in their fight to keep their land. This time, the Supreme Court ruled in favor of the Cherokee. The court said the Cherokee had the right to self-government and Georgia's state laws did not apply to them. While this sounds like a great victory, nothing changed. Georgia ignored the court's decision, and President Jackson also refused to enforce the ruling. The Cherokee were back where they started.

Meanwhile, in 1830, Jackson introduced the Indian Removal Act which was passed in Congress. Under this law, the president

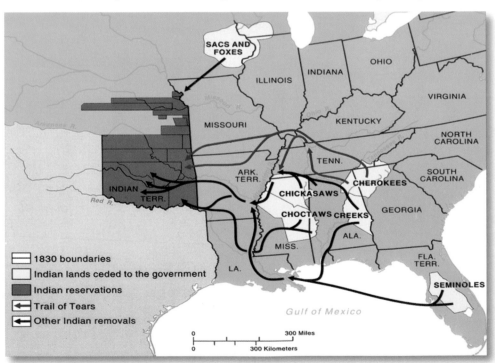

This map shows the routes taken by Native Americans who were forced from their homes by the Indian Removal Act of 1830. Natives faced brutal, deadly marches and thousands of people died before they reached their new homes in the west.

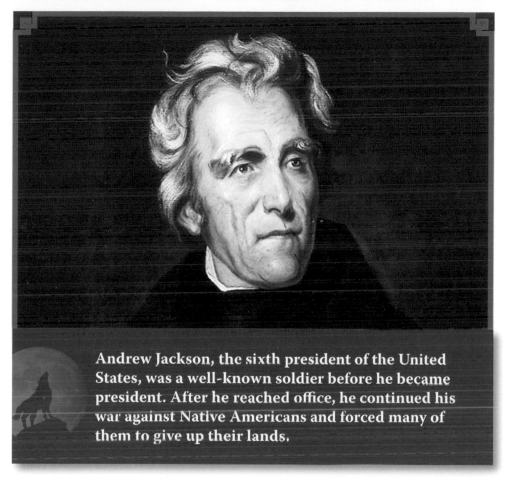

Andrew Jackson, the sixth president of the United States, was a well-known soldier before he became president. After he reached office, he continued his war against Native Americans and forced many of them to give up their lands.

could negotiate removal treaties with Indian tribes living east of the Mississippi. The Native Americans east of the Mississippi would be forced to give up their land in exchange for lands further west. Any native who wanted to stay on their land east of the Mississippi would become a citizen of the state they resided in.

It's true that Jackson wanted to get the Native Americans out of the way of American settlers. At the same time, he also believed that people would settle in eastern and southern lands anyway, and the Native Americans who stayed would be forced to live under white laws and accept white culture. To Jackson, the Indian migration to the west was going to happen no matter what.

The Trail of Tears

For the Native Americans who agreed to these treaties, their relocation was peaceful. However, when the southeastern tribes refused, Jackson turned to force. The relocation of these Native Americans was brutal and deadly. In 1838 and 1839, thousands of Cherokee were forced to march from Georgia to what is now Oklahoma. This journey became known as the Trail of Tears. About four thousand people froze to death or died of disease or starvation. Similarly, 3,500 members of the Creek tribe died on their journey from Alabama to the west. Between 1830 and 1850, about one hundred thousand Native Americans were moved into what was called "Indian Country."[1]

Life did not get much better when the Native Americans arrived in the west. The landscape and the climate were very different there. They could not grow the same crops they had grown in the east. To complicate matters, the west was already settled by other tribes; these tribes were not happy with these new arrivals moving onto their land. In addition to conflicts with Americans and the US government, the tribes were now fighting each other.

At the same time, the US government and American settlers began moving west as well. The discovery of gold in California in 1848 drew people further west; in 1869 the completion of the First Transcontinental Railroad allowed people to make the journey across the mountains and plains more easily. It wasn't long before the Native Americans' homes in the west were taken away from them too.

In 1887, Congress passed the Dawes Act. This act was meant to give individual Indians their own land rather than having them share land on a reservation. In practice, however, it allowed the

Henry Dawes was a US senator who sponsored legislation that helped the government divide land on reservations among individual Native Americans.

Soldiers guard eight Crow prisoners in Montana in 1887.

US government to assume even more control over Native Americans. Because of the Dawes Act, the Bureau of Indian Affairs was now in charge of giving out land, supervising the sale of that land, administering money belonging to Native Americans, providing health and education services to them, promoting agricultural and industrial projects to help the natives improve their land, and regulating all Indian trade. In a court case in 1903, the Supreme Court made it legal for the government to break an Indian treaty if the government believed that doing so was in the best interest of the country and the Indians. Treaties had never really protected Native American rights, but now they were officially no help at all.

Tribal governments were also in danger. After relocating to the west, many tribes, including the Creek and the Cherokee, had formed tribal governments. Then, in 1898, Congress passed the Curtis Act. This law called for the elimination of tribal governments and courts. As areas of Indian Country became US states, tribal governments also disappeared and Native Americans became citizens of the new states. Still, many Native Americans were not offered US citizenship, even after their territories became states. It wasn't until 1924 that all Native Americans living in the United States were finally granted citizenship. Despite their status as citizens, several states still continued to deny Indians the right to vote for many years.

The twentieth century saw many changes to the relationship between the Native Americans and the United States government. In 1933, John Collier was named commissioner of Indian affairs and the head of the BIA. Collier was not Native American, but

During the Oklahoma Land Rush of 1889, the government gave thousands of acres of land to settlers, who rushed into the territory to stake their claims. Before the government took it away, much of that land had belonged to native tribes.

he was a strong advocate of Native American rights. Collier quickly introduced the Indian Reorganization Act (IRA), which was passed by Congress in 1934. This act returned some land to tribal ownership and provided an additional fund for buying back Indian land. The IRA also allowed tribes to form their own governments again and provided federal money for projects that would improve the Native American economy.

Tribes were given the option to accept or reject the terms of the act. Native Americans had mixed reactions. Some natives welcomed the act, but others did not trust the US government to follow through with its promises. Other Indians preferred to become a part of American society. They did not appreciate the Bureau's view that Native Americans were somehow different from everyone else. At the same time, other American citizens felt the government should not be responsible for helping Native Americans.

Collier resigned as the head of the BIA in 1945. In 1953, a new policy called "termination" was adopted. This policy declared that "Indian tribes and individual members thereof, should be freed from Federal supervision and control."[2] Congress knew that many Indian tribes would receive millions of dollars in legal cases they had filed against the government. The government assumed the tribes could use this money to provide financial security and allow them to build businesses, create jobs, and pay taxes.

Things did not exactly work out the way Congress had expected. Even with the money from legal judgments, tribes did not have enough cash to support themselves. Some tribes had to sell land to raise money to pay their taxes. Poverty rates among Native Americans soared, and their overall quality of life declined. Despite these failures, the United States did not end the termination policy and restore tribal status and lands until 1976.

INDIAN SCHOOLS

Stewart Indian School in 1901

Between the 1880s and the 1920s, thousands of Native American children were taken away from their families and sent to boarding schools. The goal of these schools was to remove children from traditional native culture and assimilate them into white society. One of the first Indian schools was the Carlisle Indian School in Pennsylvania, which was founded by Captain Richard Henry Pratt in 1879. Pratt believed that native culture was inferior to white culture and followed the principle, "kill the Indian and save the man."[3] While most schools were run by the government, some were "mission schools" run by churches. Mission schools made it a point to teach Indians the Christian religion and forbid them from practicing native religions.

Students at Indian schools followed a strict schedule. They learned to speak English and were severely punished for speaking their native languages. Students learned basic reading, math, writing, and history. There was also a strong emphasis on vocational training. Boys performed farm chores, such as taking care of animals and planting and harvesting crops, and also learned trades such as carpentry and blacksmithing. Girls took care of chores such as laundry, cooking, and sewing, and had the opportunity to study business or nursing.

Indian schools were common until the 1920s, when it became too expensive to run them any longer. Federal reports also described inferior conditions, outbreaks of disease, and poor treatment. Indian schools were closed and by 1923, most Native American children were enrolled in regular public schools.[4]

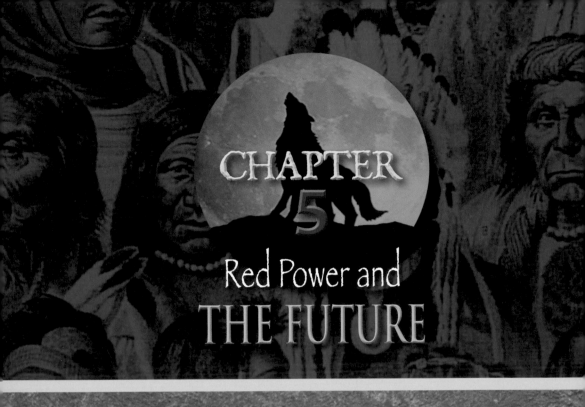

CHAPTER 5

Red Power and
THE FUTURE

The 1960s were a time of unrest in American society. Minority groups throughout the country were fighting for their rights. The Native Americans' movement was called "Red Power." In 1967, Clyde Warrior, the cofounder of the National Indian Youth Council, told the world how powerless Native Americans felt. "We are poor in spirit because we are not free—free in the most basic sense of the word," he wrote in an essay. "We are not allowed to make those basic human choices and decisions about our personal life and about the destiny of our communities which is the mark of free mature people. We sit on our front porches or in our yards, and the world and our lives in it pass us by without our desires or aspirations having any effect. We are not free. We do not make choices. Our choices are made for us; we are the poor."[1]

In 1968, President Lyndon Johnson declared that the goal of federal policy toward Native Americans had to be "a standard of living for the Indians equal to that of the country as a whole.

During Lyndon Johnson's presidency (1963-1969), he
tried to make life better for Native Americans by passing
new laws that gave them more rights and freedoms.

Freedom of choice . . . to live in equality and dignity. Full participation in the life of modern America, with a full share of economic opportunity and social justice."[2] Johnson formed the National Council on Indian Opportunity, which provided programs to assist Native Americans. In 1970, President Richard Nixon proposed that Indians take more control of their lands and the BIA interfere less in Indian affairs. Tribes were encouraged to become self-sufficient.

In 1969, Native Americans took over Alcatraz Island in the Pacific Ocean in a peaceful occupation. However, Native Americans quickly became frustrated by the lack of change. In 1972, hundreds of Native Americans traveled to Washington, DC, to protest the government's treatment of Indians. They took over BIA headquarters for seven days, but nothing changed.

Native American anger at the government reached a high point during the Red Power movement of the late 1960s and early 1970s. In 1972, hundreds of people took over the BIA's offices in Washington, DC, but their actions did little to change government treatment of native people.

AIM members and government representatives met to try to solve the violent standoff at Wounded Knee in 1973. However, their efforts were unsuccessful, and the natives surrendered and were arrested two months later.

Things turned bloody in 1973 when nearly two hundred members of an activist group called the American Indian Movement (AIM) took over the town of Wounded Knee, South Dakota. Wounded Knee was a symbolic location because it had been the site of a US Army massacre of Sioux warriors and civilians in 1890. For seventy-one days, the armed occupiers held off federal police and FBI agents. US government forces blocked off the area so people could not send in supplies such as food and ammunition. Gunfire was exchanged several times, and two Native Americans were killed. Meanwhile, the government surrounded the town with tanks and powerful ammunition, as if they were in the middle of a war. Finally, the Native American occupiers surrendered on May 8. They gave up their weapons, and many of them were arrested.

Although the siege of Wounded Knee ended in failure, it helped raise awareness among the American people about just how much the Native Americans were struggling. Government policies expressed a desire to give tribal governments more control. In 1975, Congress passed the Indian Self-Determination and Education Assistance Act. This legislation increased tribal control over their government and education. It also authorized federal money to build schools on or near Indian reservations. A few years later, in 1978, Congress passed the American Indian Religious Freedom Act. This act recognized the right of Native Americans to practice their cultural and religious traditions and beliefs and also protected their rights to access land that was considered sacred. In 1990, the Native American Graves Protection and Repatriation Act provided further protection of sacred sites and Native American burial grounds.

The government continued to give more control to tribal authorities when it passed the Tribal Self-Governance Demonstration Project in 1991. This act strengthened the Indian Self-Determination and Education Assistance Act and extended help to tribes so they could move toward self-government. Between 1990 and 1995, thirty-three Native American nations concluded the long process of creating self-government agreements with the United States. US law states that up to fifty tribes can apply for self-government every year.[3]

In November 2012, a sixteen-year court case between Native American tribes and the federal government was finally settled. This case awarded $3.4 billion to Native Americans as compensation for the US government's misuse of their land and money.

This landmark case had its beginnings in 1996, when a Blackfoot tribal leader named Elouise Cobell filed a lawsuit against the government. The US government had rented Indian land out to people who made money from the natural resources there. The government was supposed to hold money earned from the land rentals in an account for the Indians who owned that land. According to Cobell's lawsuit, that money was mismanaged and even lost by the government. The award paid individual Native Americans affected by the abuse of their lands,

President Barack Obama congratulates native activist Elouise Cobell after signing the Claims Resettlement Act in 2010. Cobell had filed her lawsuit against the government almost fifteen years earlier.

and also was used to purchase additional land for the tribe. At the time of the award, Secretary of the Interior Ken Salazar stated that "with the settlement now final, we can put years of discord behind us and start a new chapter in our nation-to-nation relationship."[4]

It remains to be seen whether Salazar's hopes will come true. Today, the US government's treatment of Native Americans has come a long way since the days of forced relocations and broken treaties. However, Native American communities are still at a terrible disadvantage compared to other parts of American

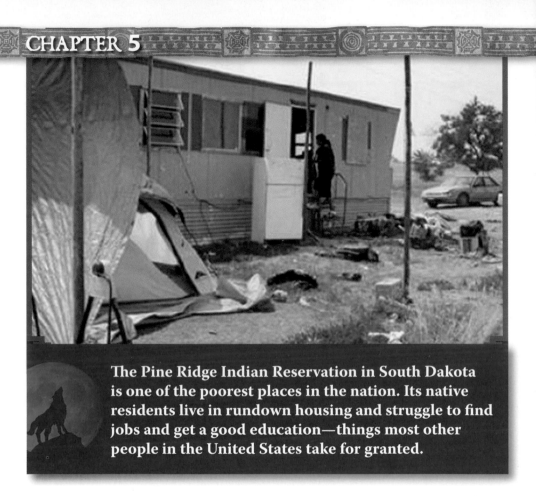

The Pine Ridge Indian Reservation in South Dakota is one of the poorest places in the nation. Its native residents live in rundown housing and struggle to find jobs and get a good education—things most other people in the United States take for granted.

society. According to the 2010 US Census, more than 28 percent of Native Americans live in poverty, compared to the national average of 15 percent. Native American youth have the highest suicide rate in the country, as well as one of the highest school dropout rates.[5] Activists point out that the United States has never compensated tribes for the millions of acres of land that were taken away from them over the years, as well as the numerous broken promises and treaties.

Will the US government and the Native American tribes ever agree on fair treatment? Unfortunately, the answer is probably not. However, we can hope that officials on both sides of the issue find a way to work together to make life better for the people whose ancestors were the first settlers of the land that is now the United States.

ARE CASINOS THE ANSWER?

As part of the move toward self-determination, Congress passed the Indian Gaming Regulatory Act, or IGRA, in 1988. This act called for the establishment of federal regulation of gambling activities on Native American land. The goal of these activities was to promote tribal development, economic self-sufficiency, and strong tribal governments. At the time, casino gambling was illegal in most parts of the United States, but it was allowed on Indian reservations. Promoters of the law wanted the government to regulate these gambling activities, to protect both Native Americans and non-native people. To achieve this, IGRA established the National Indian Gaming Commission, which monitors gambling on Native American lands.

Casinos changed Native American culture in a huge way. Suddenly, reservations located near urban centers became valuable places. Tribes built sophisticated casinos, which attracted people from the nearby areas. Casinos have allowed many tribes to prosper, providing millions of dollars in income. One of the most successful casinos is Foxwoods Resort Casino, which is located on the Mashantucket Pequot Reservation in Ledyard, Connecticut. This casino is one of the largest in the world and includes more than three hundred gaming tables and six thousand slot machines. Its location between New York City and Boston makes it a huge moneymaker for the Mashantucket Pequot tribe.

Native American casinos have become hugely popular—and a huge source of profits too.

Chapter 1:
1. Nicole Lapin and Jason Hanna, CNN, "1969 Alcatraz Take-over 'Changed the Whole Course of History,'" November 20, 2009. http://www.cnn.com/2009/CRIME/11/20/alcatraz.indian.occupation/

2. Troy R. Johnson, *The Occupation of Alcatraz Island* (Champaign, IL: Board of Trustees of the University of Illinois, 1996), p. 18.

Chapter 2:
1. Richard Harless, *The Digital Encyclopedia of George Washington,* "Native American Policy," http://www.mountvernon.org/educational-resources/encyclopedia/native-american-policy

Chapter 3:
1. Scott K. Williams, "Making Treaties: Good Faith or Deception?," January 1, 2006. http://www.usgennet.org/usa/mo/county/stlouis/native/badtreaty.htm

2. Ibid.

3. US Department of the Interior, "BIA," http://www.bia.gov/WhoWeAre/BIA/index.htm

Chapter 4:
1. National Park Service, *Trail of Tears,* "Stories," http://www.nps.gov/trte/historyculture/stories.htm

2. Charles J. Kappler, ed., *Indian Affairs: Laws and Treaties,* Volume 6 (Washington, DC: Government Printing Office), p. 614. http://digital.library.okstate.edu/kappler/Vol6/html_files/Images/v6p0614.jpg

3. Carolyn J. Marr, University of Washington, "Assimilation Through Education: Indian Boarding Schools in the Pacific Northwest," http://content.lib.washington.edu/aipnw/marr.html

4. Ibid.

Chapter 5:

1. Clyde Warrior, "We Are Not Free," http://melanconent.com/lib/oc/wearenotfree.html

2. Chris Stearns, Indian Country, "Self-Determination, LBJ and UNDRIP," May 10, 2012. http://indiancountrytodaymedianetwork.com/opinion/selfdetermination,-lbj-and-undrip-111782

3. "Part 1000—Annual Funding Agreements Under the Tribal Self-Government Act Amendments to the Indian Self-Determination and Education Act," Code of Federal Regulations (Washington, DC: US Government Printing Office, April 1, 2010). http://www.gpo.gov/fdsys/pkg/CFR-2010-title25-vol2/pdf/CFR-2010-title25-vol2-part1000.pdf

4. Matt Volz, Associated Press, "Native Americans' $3.4 Billion Lawsuit Settled, Disbursements to Begin," November 27, 2012. http://lubbockonline.com/filed-online/2012-11-27/native-americans-34-billion-lawsuitsettled-disbursements-begin#.USsa4Cc72Ag

5. Chris Stearns, Indian Country, "Self-Determination, LBJ and UNDRIP," May 10, 2012. http://indiancountrytodaymedianetwork.com/opinion/selfdetermination,-bj-and-undrip-111782

Books

Cornelissen, Cornelia. *Soft Rain: A Story of the Cherokee Trail of Tears.* New York: Yearling, 1999.

Johnson, Troy R. *Red Power: The Native American Civil Rights Movement.* New York: Chelsea House Publishers, 2007.

Stewart, Mark. *The Indian Removal Act.* Minneapolis: Compass Point Books, 2007.

Wilson, Mike. *Broken Promises: The U.S. Government and Native Americans in the 19th Century.* Broomall, PA: Mason Crest Publishers, 2002.

On the Internet:

History.com: "Native American Cultures"

http://www.history.com/topics/native-american-cultures

Oklahoma: "Oklahoma's Rich Indian History"

http://www.travelok.com/article_page/oklahomas-rich-indian-history

Works Consulted

"American Indian Movement." http://www.aimovement.org

Harless, Richard. "Native American Policy." *The Digital Encyclopedia of George Washington.* http://www.mountvernon. org/educational-resources/encyclopedia/native-american-policy

Johnson, Troy R. *The Occupation of Alcatraz Island.* Champaign, IL: Board of Trustees of the University of Illinois, 1996.

Kappler, Charles J., ed. *Indian Affairs: Laws and Treaties.* Volume 6. Washington, DC: Government Printing Office, p. 614. http:// digital.library.okstate.edu/kappler/Vol6/html_files/Images/ v6p0614.jpg

Lapin, Nicole, and Jason Hanna. "1969 Alcatraz Takeover 'Changed the Whole Course of History.'" CNN, November 20, 2009. http:// www.cnn.com/2009/CRIME/11/20/alcatraz.indian.occupation/

Marr, Carolyn J. "Assimilation Through Education: Indian Boarding Schools in the Pacific Northwest." University of Washington. http://content.lib.washington.edu/aipnw/marr.html

Michigan State University Library. "AIM and Wounded Knee Documents." http://www.aics.org/WK/index.html

National Park Service. "Stories." *Trail of Tears.* http://www.nps.gov/trte/historyculture/stories.htm

"Part 1000—Annual Funding Agreements Under the Tribal Self-Government Act Amendments to the Indian Self-Determination and Education Act." Code of Federal Regulations, Washington, DC: US Government Printing Office, April 1, 2010. http://www.gpo.gov/fdsys/pkg/CFR-2010-title25-vol2/pdf/CFR-2010-title25-vol2-part1000.pdf

PBS. "Indian Removal." *Africans in America.* http://www.pbs.org/wgbh/aia/part4/4p2959.html

Stearns, Chris. "Self-Determination, LBJ and UNDRIP." Indian Country, May 10, 2012. http://indiancountrytodaymedianetwork.com/opinion/self-determination,-lbj-and-undrip-111782

US Department of the Interior. "BIA." http://www.bia.gov/WhoWeAre/BIA/index.htm

Volz, Matt. "Native Americans' $3.4 Billion Lawsuit Settled, Disbursements to Begin." Associated Press, November 27, 2012. http://lubbockonline.com/filed-online/2012-11-27/native-americans-34-billion-lawsuit-settled-disbursements-begin#.USsa4Cc72Ag

Warrior, Clyde. "We Are Not Free." http://melanconent.com/lib/oc/wearenotfree.html

Williams, Scott K. "Making Treaties: Good Faith or Deception?" January 1, 2006. http://www.usgennet.org/usa/mo/county/stlouis/native/badtreaty.htm

Winton, Ben. "Alcatraz, Indian Land." *Native Peoples Magazine,* Fall 1999. http://siouxme.com/lodge/alcatraz_np.html

advocate (AD-vuh-kit): someone who defends the cause of another

assimilate (uh-SIM-uh-lait): to become part of another culture

blockade (blah-KEYD): to block or surround a place in order to prevent people or supplies from passing in or out

bribe (BRAHYB): money or favors given to persuade someone to do something

casualties (KAZH-yoo-uhl-tees): people killed or injured in battle

consistent (kuhn-SIS-tuhnt): working the same way or following the same rules every time

corruption (kuh-RUP-shuhn): dishonest or unlawful behavior

enhance (en-HANS): to make better or improve the value of

legislate (LEJ-uhs-lait): to put into law

massacre (MASS-uh-ker): the killing of a large number of people

migration (my-GRAY-shuhn): the movement of a large number of people or animals to a new location

missionary (MISH-uh-nair-ee): a person sent by a religious organization to promote its beliefs and do good works

negotiate (nih-GOH-shee-ate): to talk to another in order to come to an agreement on an issue

nomad (NOH-mad): a person who travels from place to place and has no permanent home

occupation (ok-yoo-PAY-shuhn): the seizure and control of an area by force

plight (PLAHYT): an unfortunate situation

policy (PAHL-uh-see): a defined method or course of action used by a government or organization

reservation (rez-er-VAY-shuhn): public land set aside for use by a specific group such as Native Americans

seminal (SEM-uh-nuhl): original, something that inspires future developments

sovereign (SOHV-rihn): having supreme power and authority

termination (ter-muh-NAY-shuhn): ending

treaty (TREE-tee): an agreement between two or more nations